FOUNDING PATRON

The listed plane tree, which has marked the entrance to The Dorchester since the hotel opened its doors in 1931,
was designated one of the Great Trees of London by Trees for Cities in 1997

The Dorchester

GOLD PATRONS

The Camelot Group of Companies

City of London Corporation

The Hearst Corporation

Jaguar Land Rover

Kent & Curwen

HSBC

UPS

SILVER PATRONS

Anglo American

Berkeley Group

Brassington Chartering

Carol Joy London

Catlin Group
(Speciality Insurance)

Compass Group
UK & Ireland Ltd

Constantia-Hellenic
Real Estate, Monaco

Delancey

De La Rue plc

Edgerton Distillers

ExxonMobil

Farrer & Co LLP

Foyles Bookshop

Holiday Property Bond

Jones Lang LaSalle

Lloyds TSB
Private Banking

L'Oréal UK & Ireland

Marlon Abela
Restaurant Corporation

Marshall of Cambridge

Merrill Lynch
Wealth Management

Nomura

Populous

Rio Tinto

Royal Bank of Canada
Wealth Management

SAMM Financial Monaco

Silversea Cruises

SOP International

Vodafone

BRONZE PATRONS

PRIVATE PATRONS

THE SPIRIT
OF
LONDON

ANTHONY OSMOND-EVANS

THE BEAUTIFUL PUBLISHING COMPANY

FOREWORD

The Mayor of London
Boris Johnson

Welcome to London, proud host of the 2012 Olympic and Paralympic Games.

We Londoners hold our city to be, quite simply, the best big city in the world, and have always extended a warm welcome to people from every country, every continent, to make London their home. And we will do so with even more vigour this year.

In London you will discover a city of diversity, contrasts and contradictions. A sprawling metropolis, encompassing more green space, parks and waterways than any comparable city; historic buildings jostling with cutting-edge architecture; old-style charm and quality meet world-leading innovation, technology and design. More than 300 languages are now spoken in the city, more than 27 faiths and religions are practised. Fifty of the Olympic and Paralympic teams who arrive in London this year will be greeted by 'home crowds' of tens of thousands of their own nation already living here.

And London is a giant transport hub: every year over 100 million passengers travel through our four international airports and over 250 million use our public transport.

London is home to a diverse, thriving economy. A global centre of the financial, legal, advertising, accounting and insurance sectors, London also has one of the most vibrant cultural and creative sectors in the world: theatre, music, art, architecture, fashion and film production attract talent and audiences from every continent. And there is sport for all to enjoy: cricket at Lord's and The Oval; football at Wembley, rugby at Twickenham; tennis at Wimbledon, rowing and sailing on the River Thames.

From this diversity, rooted in a strong sense of our shared history, both ancient and modern, springs the unique spirit of London: a spirit that strives to be the best, that celebrates fair play, that seeks to create a level playing field for all comers. And it is this spirit that I hope you will have a chance to experience as you participate in the 2012 Olympics and Paralympics.

Maybe it is this readiness to rise to a challenge that led London to seek to host the 2012 Olympics Games. And by doing so, London itself becomes something of an Olympic record-breaker: the only city ever to have hosted the event three times – 1908, 1948 and 2012. In 1908 we stepped in at the last minute as an alternative venue to Rome following the eruption of Mount Vesuvius. Those Games fondly remembered in Britain as the first – and so far only – time that we have topped the medal table.

Once again, in 1948, we came to the rescue and at short notice hosted the first Games after the Second World War. Post-war austerity meant that athletes stayed in military barracks and – with rationing still in place – many teams had to bring their own food. We can promise a higher degree of comfort and cuisine in 2012.

This time we have had rather longer to prepare, and I have watched with pride and excitement as the dream nurtured for well over a decade by a small group of residents in East London has become the London 2012 Olympic and Paralympic Games. As magnificent structures have risen above what was, for generations, a blighted part of this great city. And as thousands of new jobs and homes have been created. An Olympic legacy has been forged, which will last long after the greatest show on earth has come to an end.

It is with humility that I reflect on what London, in turn, has bequeathed to the Olympic movement. The marathon distance of 26.2 miles was established in 1908 because it was the distance between Windsor Castle and the Royal Box at the Olympic Stadium in White City. The Paralympics themselves were heralded in 1948, when the first archery event for injured soldiers was held at Stoke Mandeville Hospital. Also, the 1948 Olympic Games were the first to feature the volunteer programmes, which now

Opposite: Boris Johnson, Mayor of London, is also a classical scholar. Pictured here with the bronze head of his hero, Emperor Augustus

Above: The Eurostar terminal at St Pancras connects London with Paris and Brussels and onward to other European cities

enable Olympic host cities to offer such a warm welcome to the athletes and visitors arriving for the Games – and which we anticipate will mobilise over 100,000 volunteers in 2012.

As we celebrate this wonderful six-week festival of sport, however, I confess to feeling some relief that one standard set in 1908 has not survived the intervening century: back then, the Games lasted six months!

To augment this already heightened sense of celebration, 2012 is also the year of the Diamond Jubilee of the reign of our Sovereign, Queen Elizabeth II. Her indomitable spirit has steered the helm of our nation throughout the 60 years of her reign. A period that has encompassed the London fashion boom of the racy 1960s, the 1980s' Big Bang, and Cool Britannia in the 1990s.

London welcomes the world and opens its doors to people of every nationality to come and share in the spirit of our magnificent capital city. The eyes of the world are on London once again, so what better way to celebrate our capital city than with this splendid tome. This book *The Spirit of London* is the perfect embodiment of old and new, London now and then, the people, the cultures, the vibrancy and the most wonderful sporting showcase on earth – the Olympic Games.

CITY OF LONDON

FOREWORD

The Right Honourable The Lord Mayor of the City of London

Alderman David Wootton

The Olympic and Paralympic Games will make 2012 a landmark year for London and it is a great opportunity for me that the Games fall during my year of office.

I am delighted that the City of London Corporation, which as Lord Mayor I head, is supporting this excellent publication, *The Spirit of London*. The book offers a special way for our visitors to remember these Games through photographs which show the sheer variety on display in today's London – people, places, work and play. The City Corporation is committed to supporting the Games fully throughout the coming year across a variety of sporting and cultural activities, and the Square Mile will be a gateway for many of the events.

But I also believe in the many benefits that sport can provide, having been a keen sportsman myself in younger days. At Jesus College, Cambridge, I captained its First Boat in 1972 when the crew swept the board against all comers. Sport is a chance both for individual achievement and to excel as part of a team.

And the themes underlying the Games apply just as well to the Square Mile itself: the competitive environment, the drive to succeed, the search for the best talent and the opportunity for all, regardless of background. The City is a world leader in international finance and business services because of its people: their hard work, innovation and enthusiasm. The Olympic ethos is alive and well in the City every working day.

Momentous events like the Games can also draw people together. During the six-week period in 2012 I am sure we will all see and feel the genuine 'spirit of London', as we become caught up in the anticipation, excitement and achievement. It will be a special time for us and one that few will forget.

In support of the wider work of the City Corporation, as Lord Mayor it is my job to promote the City on the world stage as a centre of excellence in which to do business. The Olympic and Paralympic Games, with their huge influx of visitors and media attention, can only help in that task. The world's attention will be on London and it will be an ideal time to showcase exactly what the capital has to offer. I will be looking to use this to encourage inward investment, trade and business location here. The spotlight of the world will be upon us and we should make the most of it.

We should also look to build on the success of the Games so that their impact lasts well beyond the Closing Ceremony. London's bid to host the Games was boosted by the many economic benefits that they would offer to all of London and by the prospect of social and cultural legacy. The effects can already be seen in the huge infrastructure improvements, investment and employment that have taken place in order to cope with the scale of the Games. We must build on these to ensure future prosperity and benefits to all our lives.

The Olympic and Paralympic Games are a once-in-a-lifetime opportunity to show London at its best. We must seize this and use it as a springboard for future success.

Opposite: The Silent Ceremony at Guildhall. All incoming Lord Mayors of the City of London are formally admitted to office in November on the Friday prior to the Lord Mayor's Show. Here Alderman David Wootton, Lord Mayor 2011–2012, processes to make his declaration of office before the Aldermen and Sheriffs, and receive the City insignia from the outgoing Lord Mayor, Sir Michael Bear. Nothing else is said, hence the ceremony's name

INTRODUCTION
Anthony Osmond-Evans

It was as a 19-year-old articled accountant back in the sixties that I took 'swinging London' to my heart when I first lived there and commuted to the City each day, wearing a bowler hat and carrying a deftly-furled umbrella.

Having since lived much of my adult life overseas, photographing in lands as far-flung as Tibet, returning to London is always a huge pleasure. As someone who delights in capturing the visual image, I feel most fortunate to have been given this opportunity by our Patrons both to indulge my passion for photography and to re-visit my favourite city.

It has been 12 years since the publication of my book, *Britain: The Book of The Millennium*, and I have discovered in London a city which, during the last decade, has grown markedly in confidence, creativity and diversity.

2012 is the year London is to be honed and polished and shown in all her finery. Not only does the city host the Olympics and Paralympics, but it is also the Diamond Jubilee of HM Queen Elizabeth II, who has served our nation selflessly and with steadfast devotion for 60 years. This will be celebrated in June with a 1,000-strong flotilla heading down the River Thames past the Tower of London.

So 2012 is the ideal opportunity for me to publish a memorable book of my photographic impressions. It has been both a challenge and a joy putting together the final selection. London's pageantry and ceremony, such as the Lord Mayor's Banquet at Guildhall, and its unique vistas – especially when lit by the dawn sun from the east – have once again woven their magic. I trust you will discover the same on the pages of this book.

The spirit of London is a broad concept that perfectly fits the ethos of the 2012 Olympic and Paralympic Games and is reflected in the words of Baron de Coubertin, the founder of the modern Olympics: 'The most important thing in the Olympic Games is not winning but taking part; the essential thing in life is not conquering but fighting

well.' In recent times, two former England cricket captains, Lord (Colin) Cowdrey and Ted Dexter, caused a similar ideal, 'The Spirit of Cricket', to be enshrined in the Rules of Cricket.

London, this year, is also hosting a Cultural Olympiad headed by Lord (Tony) Hall, which includes special events in theatre, music and the arts. Since the time of Shakespeare there has been no better place than London for theatre. Today, opera, classical music, pop concerts and film command huge audiences. But we should not forget that singular talent can be found in lesser-known haunts as diverse as Ronnie Scott's jazz club in Soho and the free lunchtime classical performances at many of our places of worship.

I love the spontaneity of London. Recently, for example, after an exceptionally sensitive performance by Natalie Clein and the National Youth Orchestra of Elgar's Cello Concerto – a particular favourite of mine – the audience was thrilled when the 150 young musicians downed their instruments and gave a brilliant 'surprise' interpretation of the Maori haka war dance from New Zealand.

Throughout London adventurous young chefs are opening superb new restaurants with delicious dishes from all over the world. Soho's delicatessens emit the pungent whiff of roasted coffee beans and exotic spices. London's markets provide the finest produce, from meat at centuries-old Smithfield to fruit and vegetables at the new Covent Garden and fish at vibrant Billingsgate in Docklands.

I could not have produced this book without the generous support of our Patrons. They have enabled me to provide copies of this book for the Mayor of London to present as a gift to the Olympian and Paralympian competitors. Many of the Patrons have made their own individual or corporate contribution to the rich tapestry of London's life. So many have given me advice, help and

encouragement personally. To all our Patrons I would like to especially extend my most heartfelt and sincere thanks.

It is my profound wish that *The Spirit of London,* for decades to come, will be a treasured memory of 2012, a unique and very special year in our great city of London.

Anthony Osmond-Evans
London, April 2012

John Walker & Sons, Scotch Whisky Distillers by Appointment to Her Majesty The Queen, is celebrating her Diamond Jubilee with a remarkable luxury Blended Scotch Whisky. A blend of whiskies from 1952, Diamond Jubilee by John Walker & Sons was finished in casks of English oak from the Sandringham Estate and bottled 60 years to the day HM Queen Elizabeth II acceded to the throne. (Photo courtesy of John Walker & Sons)

THE HISTORY OF LONDON

50	Londinium established by the Romans
61	Queen Boadicea destroys London
886	London becomes capital of England
1066	William I crowned at Westminster Abbey
1197	Henry Fitz-Alwyn first Mayor of London
1209	London Bridge. Only Thames bridge until 1739
1241	First Parliament established at Westminster
1348	Black Death kills one third of the population
1381	Peasants' Revolt storms London
1397	Sir Richard (Dick) Whittington made Lord Mayor
1476	William Caxton – first London printing press
1534	Henry VIII's divorce. Church of England established
1556–1603	Reign of Queen Elizabeth I
1599	William Shakespeare's Globe Theatre opens
1600	The East India Company established
1603–1625	Reign of King James I
1605	Gunpowder Plot fails to blow up Parliament
1642	Civil War – Parliamentarians defeat Royalists
1660	Restoration of the monarchy
1665	Great Plague of London
1666	Great Fire of London
1694	Bank of England established
1708	Wren completes St Paul's Cathedral
1714	First Georgian monarch
1773	Stock Exchange founded
1829	Peel creates Metropolitan Police
1837–1901	Reign of Queen Victoria
1851	Great Exhibition in Hyde Park
1863	Metropolitan line, world's first underground railway
1881	Savoy Theatre, first to be lit by electric light
1884	Greenwich Meridian made global standard
1908	First London Olympic Games
1914–1918	First World War
1922	First BBC radio broadcast
1939–1945	Second World War. London Blitz kills 20,000
1948	Second London Olympic Games
1951	Festival of Britain, Great Exhibition centenary
1952–	Reign of Queen Elizabeth II
1966	England win football World Cup, Wembley
1999	London Eye launched
2000	Ken Livingstone elected first Mayor of London
2012	Third London Olympics Queen Elizabeth II's Diamond Jubilee

Opposite: Harrods, the department store in Knightsbridge, before the First World War. Cromwell Road was as crowded then with horse-drawn carriages as it is today with luxury cars

MY LONDON

Clemency Burton-Hill

When people ask me where I'm from, my answer is as instinctive to me as breathing. *London*. I am from London, born and bred, and I have always felt like one of the world's lucky people because of that.

On my wedding day a few years ago, I beeped my Oyster card onto the District Line at Putney Bridge and disembarked a little over six miles east along the river, at Temple. On what should have been one of the most anxiety-inducing mornings of my life, I remember dancing along the Strand with an overwhelming sense of being accompanied by the greatest friend a girl could have. I was getting married in a church so bursting with London history it was almost mind-boggling – from the Knights Templar to the *Da Vinci Code* – and for that reason alone it should have been somewhat daunting. But with London as my oldest and dearest ally to guide my way, it simply became another exciting adventure.

Perhaps every single day in this city is an adventure. How to explain the pulsing of the blood, the quickening of the heart, the smile that can't be stopped as I cross Waterloo Bridge from North to South, wondering whether the view to my left or right is more breathtaking? How to convey the sense of expectation as I skip up the stairs of the 22 bus towards Piccadilly to my favourite seat – right at the very front, where I can watch the city go about her multi-farious business beneath me? Or describe the singular pleasure of buying a steaming cup of tea and a bacon roll at the crack of dawn at Borough Market?

The excitement as I cross Floral Street into the murmuring foyer of the Royal Opera House, or take my seat at a West End theatre opening on Shaftesbury Avenue, or spend a summer 'Promenading' every night at Kensington's Albert Hall to the world's finest orchestras and soloists for a fiver? The gratitude as I simply pop in, on a whim, on a lunch break, to freely behold some of humankind's greatest works of art at the National Gallery,

the Tate, the Royal Academy? How blessed am I, to be able to shuffle down the footsteps of world history as I steal through the cloisters of Westminster Abbey, along the hidden corridor that connects my old school, founded by Elizabeth I, to the Abbey itself; or celebrate Christmas Eve by candlelight in the Tower of London's bloodstained little church? What about the surge of adrenaline as I used to move as one with the crowd pouring out of Arsenal Tube station and up Gillespie Road at 2.45pm on a Saturday afternoon; or watch England take a wicket at Lord's; or cheer the winning ace served at Wimbledon?

What fun, to trawl for antiques on Portobello Road or in Bermondsey Market and toast any treasures with a pint of London Pride at a public house that's probably as old as the city itself! And how to express the calm that descends as I jog along the towpath of the Thames at Hammersmith, dusk falling, the fairy-lights of London's bridges twinkling in the distance? The joy and the wonder as a shaft of sunlight dazzles the stones of Big Ben and the Houses of Parliament, rendering them – and all the extraordinary stories contained within them – a shimmer of gold? The sense of sheer good fortune as I clamber over Hampstead Heath up to Parliament Hill, lines of Keats in my head, a refrain of Handel in there too? How not to take for granted the fact I might just as easily dash into the British Library and view works of Shakespeare in quarto as I may sit in his theatre, The Globe, and watch his plays burst back into life more than four centuries later, as exhilarating and relevant as ever?

Oh, London, what an embarrassment of riches, that I might hear ten of your orchestras, visit fifty of your theatres, support five of your major football teams, visit a hundred of your galleries and museums (all proving your eternally curious embrace of *everything*), see your four World Heritage Sites, marvel at your world-defining buildings, enjoy your gazillion different cuisines, hear the

Borough Market is a popular haunt for tourists and discerning 'foodies'. Based in Southwark, it is thought to date back to at least 1014. It began primarily selling fruit and vegetables but today sells all manner of British and international produce

chatter of your three hundred languages in these most beloved streets.

Cut my veins and I will bleed the Thames.

To belong here – to be able to call *this* place home – I think just might be one of the greatest privileges on earth. But you don't need to have been born here to be a Londoner, and that's what makes this city most special of all.

This summer we open our arms to the world in the free spirit of the Olympic and Paralympic Games.

For over a millennium, London has been so much more than just England's capital. She is a truly internationalist, open-eyed, open-hearted city, and remains so: more international visitors come here than to any other city in the world, and many of them stay forever. I sometimes wonder how it is possible that each pocket of the city can have such

a distinctive flavour and yet the identity of the city remains so overwhelmingly Londonish. Brixton, say, is as distinct – culturally, demographically, socially, architecturally, politically – from Primrose Hill as Primrose Hill is from Greenwich, or Mayfair, Chiswick, Westminster, Hampstead, Soho, Spitalfields, Covent Garden, Little Venice, Richmond, Islington, Westbourne Park, Bloomsbury, Chelsea, and the East End... And yet, all these areas are inescapably, magnificently London. I hope you will have the chance to visit them all and see for yourself.

In a spirit of humility and humanity – a spirit that has always coursed through the heart of this miraculous, multi-faceted, multi-cultural city – I say: London is the party, and the whole world is invited.

Welcome.

THE EAST INDIA COMPANY

The Honourable Merchants of London

A native of Mumbai, India, Sanjiv Mehta is proud to have adopted London to enable him to restore the global trading fortunes of The East India Company – once Britain's oldest and most powerful global trader. During its heyday, The East India Company not only established trade through Asia and the Middle East, but also effectively became the ruler of territories vastly larger than the United Kingdom itself.

'There is no place where I can live and work more freely than in London,' observes Mehta. Today his Company's products, including spiced teas, biscuits, marmalades, mustards, chocolates and salts – each exquisitely produced and packaged to meticulous formulae – can be found in the magic of The East India Company shop on the corner of London's Regent and Conduit Streets.

The Company has also partnered with the Royal Mint, re-establishing a relationship many centuries old. For the first time in 150 years the Royal Mint has struck East India Company gold, creating a coin inspired by the 'Mohur', once the trading currency of The Company.

When founded by Royal Charter on the very last day of 1600 in the declining years of the reign of Queen Elizabeth I, it was known as *The Governor and Company of Merchants of London Trading into the East Indies*. As its name suggests, The Company was the enterprise of London businessmen who banded together to make money importing sought-after spices from South Asia.

A captivating tale. The first merchants of The East India Company ventured forth in 1601 from the hallowed hall of The Worshipful Company of Skinners. The Company's pioneers founded the great trading ports of Mumbai and Hong Kong. Its teas were 'served' at the Boston Tea Party, and its intriguing imports of teas, spices and delicate cloth delighted the gentry across the British Empire. The East India Company has connected the world in myriad ways and its influence on London and the British Commonwealth is unparalleled.

London, the nation's capital, is the centre of the world's financial markets and commerce, fashioned from centuries of global trade. The City of London's livery companies reflect the uncompromising standards of their crafts – and created the foundation of trust through which trade could be conducted with confidence. The London Stock Exchange's motto, 'Dictum Meum Pactum' – 'My Word is My Bond' – is the gold standard of spoken trading integrity and precedes the written contracts provided by the army of London's legal services, upon which international trading depends today.

London's diversity of cultures from around the globe, amidst Britain's own rich history and heritage, is embedded in British democracy and rule of law, which provide the stable platform for people to live and work peaceably in London. This all makes for the greatness of a city – uniquely, London – which now plays such an important and significant role in Sanjiv Mehta's own admirable life journey.

Opposite: The East India Company's sumptuous flagship store on Mayfair's Conduit Street, inspired by the Company's rich legacy, provides the finest teas, chocolates and epicurean treasures

The Men's 100 Metres Final at Wembley Stadium
during the London 1948 Olympic Games

LONDON 1948 OLYMPICS:
AN UNSUNG HERO

Charles Woodhouse CVO DL
A retired partner of Farrer & Co

In December 1945, a small tight-knit group of well-connected sportsmen was convened by the British Olympic Association (BOA) honorary secretary, Colonel Evan Hunter. At a time of post-war austerity their purpose was to reconstitute the BOA council and consider whether London should stage the 1948 Olympics. One of that group was Emrys Lloyd, the BOA honorary legal adviser, who after distinguished war service had just re-joined his eminent London law firm, Farrer & Co. Lloyd was a seven times British fencing champion who represented Great Britain in four Olympic Games.

The group included two International Olympic Committee (IOC) members, Lord Aberdare and Sir Noel Curtis-Bennett, and two future presidents of international sports federations, Stanley Rous – football, and Harold Fern – swimming. They reported to Lord Burghley (later Marquess of Exeter), then BOA chairman, who was for many years vice-president of the IOC. Lloyd and Burghley were both born in 1905 and had been close friends since Cambridge in the 1920s.

Both had been selected for the Amsterdam 1928 Olympics, but whilst Lloyd was unable to attend because of final exams, Burghley won gold in the hurdles. Both took part in the Los Angeles Olympics in 1932. Emrys Lloyd came fifth in the foil and, astonishingly, doubled up as reserve cox for the rowing eight.

The managing director of Wembley stadium, Arthur Elvin, repeated Wembley's earlier offer to stage the Games. All Wembley wanted, he said, was the honour of being associated with the first post-war Games, with no desire for profit. Emrys Lloyd was detailed to liaise with Arthur Elvin, and the BOA reached its decision in spring 1946.

Lloyd insisted that the BOA should form an organising committee as a separate company, limited by guarantee to avoid the risk of personal liability and to prevent any misapprehension that it was being formed with a profit motive. This became known as 'The Organising Committee for the XIVth Olympiad London'. Lloyd's model has been followed for all subsequent Games.

Lloyd wrote 'no charge' on his letters. His law firm, Farrer & Co, after more than a year's professional work for the organising committee, were warmly thanked for their 'generous gesture' in limiting their costs to two hundred guineas (£210).

In the two years before the Games, Lloyd put together scores of contracts for venues, suppliers and sponsors. Crucially, given the absence of government funding, Wembley provided a guarantee against loss, and a cash advance to be recouped from ticket sales.

Emrys Lloyd was unique in the history of the Olympics, both for setting up the organising committee and then competing in the same Games.

Lloyd carried the British flag at the 1948 Opening Ceremony. He had mislaid his British team beret, on which he had been sitting, and so led out the British team hatless on a scorching day in front of King George VI.

Lloyd and Burghley, quintessential amateurs both, lived to see the day when in 1981 the IOC opened the way to professionals. There was no longer need to be, or pretend to be, an amateur. It was another era far removed from 1948. So too will be this third London Olympics of 2012. But at the opening ceremony hats (or berets) should be doffed in memory of Lloyd and his splendid BOA colleagues who saved and continued the Olympic Games.

The Peacock Room at the Royal solicitors, Farrer & Co, where the Olympic Bond was signed in 1948 and the Bank of England Charter in 1694. On the walls are portraits, some by Romney, of past Farrers' partners. Charles Dickens was a notable client

LONDON ON THE COUCH

Lucy Beresford

The character of the Londoner has long been examined, epitomized by the cheeky chappie cockney or the spirit of the Blitz evoked during World War II. But what of the psyche of the city itself? What would we find if we put London on the couch?

Like any thorough psychoanalysis, attention must be paid to the past: to London's civic history. Old street names such as Poultry, Cloth Fair or Cheapside (from the Saxon *ceap*, to barter) remind us for example of a city long fuelled by commercial energy. Over the centuries, as London became both national capital and centre of the royal court, it revealed itself to be a can-do city, enjoying prestige, favour and prosperity.

This is partly because, psychologically, London possesses a highly adaptive personality. For centuries, people have been drawn to the banks of the Thames from all over the world, with Romans, Vikings, and Normans being just some of the earliest examples. Over time, this diversity has required high levels of what psychologists call social adjustment. Tolerance and accommodation have been the city's watchwords.

However, the human brain is not able to cope with too many diverse networks. We thrive best in units of around 150 people – the size of a village. And so, while London has grown in size and complexity, the social relationships of the village, or even the street, have instinctively been retained in the unconscious. London remains a series of villages – linked together like pearls on a necklace. Whether it's Bethnal Green, Hounslow, Soho, Kensington, Notting Hill or Pimlico, each area provides a distinct thread which contributes to the texture of the tolerant whole. There's an almost quixotic single-mindedness about a city which is both proud to be one and yet which has managed to retain an atmosphere of exquisite intimacy.

This concept of the 'village' gives London its ego strength. It is a grounded city, proud of its past, not trying to be something it isn't. Such ego strength makes London also a brave city, unafraid to experiment, to grow, to flex its muscles in the international ring. Born on a major river, commerce and trade flood through its veins, providing employment and social stability for its inhabitants. With the seafaring port firmly in its DNA, London is today home to an increasingly diverse range of cultures, cuisines, races and faiths. Over 300 languages are spoken within its boundaries.

To some, it's a wonder that London functions as well as it does. It is too sprawling, too old, too muddled. And it has known periods of self-doubt. Like The Six Jolly Fellowship Porters, the pub mentioned in Dickens's paean to London – his novel *Our Mutual Friend* – some feel London might very soon topple over into the Thames. Or implode.

Yet the beauty, the wonder, the thrill of London is that it functions, that it thrives, in spite of its major design flaws. Alongside a certain stoicism – a 'bloody but not bowed' Bulldog tenacity – we find London's compassion and agreeableness. Over the centuries, it has known what it means to be attacked, to be invaded, to be violated. And yet out of this comes its willingness to absorb 'the outsider', and to learn from its own mistakes. It is a city of empathy, providing shelter to those in need. It is a city which understands explicitly what it means to have to start all over again.

In the future, such openness to experience will continue to be the defining personality trait of a city still enlivened by regeneration. Above all, it is a city which refuses to be stereotyped.

And not surprisingly, it is this which has made London one of the most admired, most loved, most inspiring cities in the world.

Opposite: Berry Bros. & Rudd, Britain's oldest wine and spirit merchant. Established in 1698, it is still family-run. Supplier to the Royal Family since George III's reign (1760–1820). It has been a tradition to weigh customers on the great scale (front). Famous names in the weight book include the Prince Regent, Lord Byron and the Duke of Wellington

A CABBIE'S LONDON KNOWLEDGE

David Styles

As any artist, writer or photographer will tell you, they will observe the world around them in ways that others might take for granted. It is that same attention to detail that is needed when one undertakes 'The Knowledge', the qualification required to become a London cabbie. Every street, club, bar, church, hotel and even blue plaque must be committed to memory. In pursuit of all these facets of London – more than 25,000 individual details – the 'Knowledge' student discovers that there is more to London than is apparent at first sight.

The 'Knowledge' was introduced in 1851 after complaints by visitors to the Great Exhibition that cabbies did not know where they were going. Now after 160 years we are regarded as the world's finest taxi service. But our pedigree goes back even further; London was the first city in the world to have a licensed taxi trade, which can be blamed on the great 16th-century playwright, William Shakespeare. His plays were so popular that all the carriages arriving to pick up and drop off the theatre-going public would cause a 'stop' – in modern day parlance a traffic jam. It took the authorities about 40 years after Shakespeare's death to introduce licensing. In 1654 the City of London authorised the use of 200 licenses for Hackney coachmen.

With such a long history it is hardly surprising that anachronisms abound in the cab trade. The modern cab has a high roof so that gentlemen wearing top hats may leave them on when travelling to Ascot. A cabbie was required to carry sufficient hard food for his horse's midday meal. This is now interpreted as having a boot large enough to take a bale of hay. In time of need, a cabbie may urinate over his

rear nearside wheel provided a police constable is in attendance to protect his modesty by shielding him with a police cape. Should he wish to stop at a Cabbies' Green Shelter, he may eat and drink tea, but 'political discussion' is forbidden by the Victorian philanthropists who originally donated the shelters.

While studying the 'Knowledge', a student discovers that some streets in the City – Milk Street, Goldsmith Street, Ironmonger Lane – are named after the goods once sold there; or that Old Jewry was an area set aside for Jewish money lenders. As for the tradition of the London Stone located in Cannon Street, a little research suggests that London's prosperity for many years was thought to depend on the Stone's safekeeping. The Romans could have used this limestone block as the point from which to measure all distances from Londinium.

The words of Dr Samuel Johnson should be the mantra for any prospective 'Knowledge' student:

> 'Sir, if you wish to have a just notion of the magnitude of this city, you must not be satisfied with seeing its great streets and squares, but must survey the innumerable little lanes and courts. It is not in the showy evolutions of buildings, but in the multiplicity of human habitations which are crowded together, that the wonderful immensity of London consists.'

Right: Relaxing with a cup of tea and a newspaper in a London café

Opposite: Cabmen's shelter at Albert Bridge, Chelsea. In 1874 Lord Shaftesbury set up a fund to provide shelters offering horse-drawn Hackney Carriage drivers 'wholesome refreshments at moderate prices'. By 1914 there were 61 green huts; today only 13 remain

Three beauties in London. Top left: Annabel Pugh

Top right: Heather Acheson, who works for HSH Prince Albert II of Monaco, a member of the IOC, on a visit to The Dorchester Spa

Below: Peanut, a miniature dachshund in the arms of Russian model, Ivgenia

Opposite: The head chef Chi Leung at the Grand Imperial London Chinese restaurant in Victoria prepares classical Cantonese delicacies to accompany his signature lobster and abalone masterpieces. A lobster in Chinese is called a dragon prawn – and 2012 is the Chinese Year of the Dragon, the most important in the Chinese calendar

Top left: Chief Rabbi Lord (Jonathan) Sacks in his St John's Wood garden. He has been head of the United Hebrew Congregations of the Commonwealth since 1991

Top right: Dan Stevens. He plays Matthew Crawley, handsome heir to the estate in *Downton Abbey*, the much-acclaimed TV series written by Julian Fellowes

Below: David Beckham, legendary England football captain

Opposite top: Lord Chief Justice Igor Judge and Master of the Rolls, Lord Neuberger, with their wives, arriving at the annual Lord Mayor's Banquet at Guildhall

Opposite below: David and Simon Reuben with their wives Debra and Joyce have been substantial donors to the Great Ormond Street Hospital by creating the Reuben Foundation Children's Cancer Centre. In the background, a portrait of Princess Victoria Mary, daughter of King George V

Following page: Crocuses in the spring at Hampton Court. Sir Christopher Wren designed this 18th-century wing of the Palace for King William III. It was an extension to the original Tudor palace of Cardinal Wolsey acquired by King Henry VIII in 1529

Daffodils at the Animals in War Memorial, Park Lane. A tribute to all animals that served, suffered and died alongside the British, Commonwealth and Allied forces in wars and conflicts of the 20th century. The inscription 'They had no choice' was written by military historian Leo Cooper, husband of novelist Jilly Cooper, a Trustee of the memorial

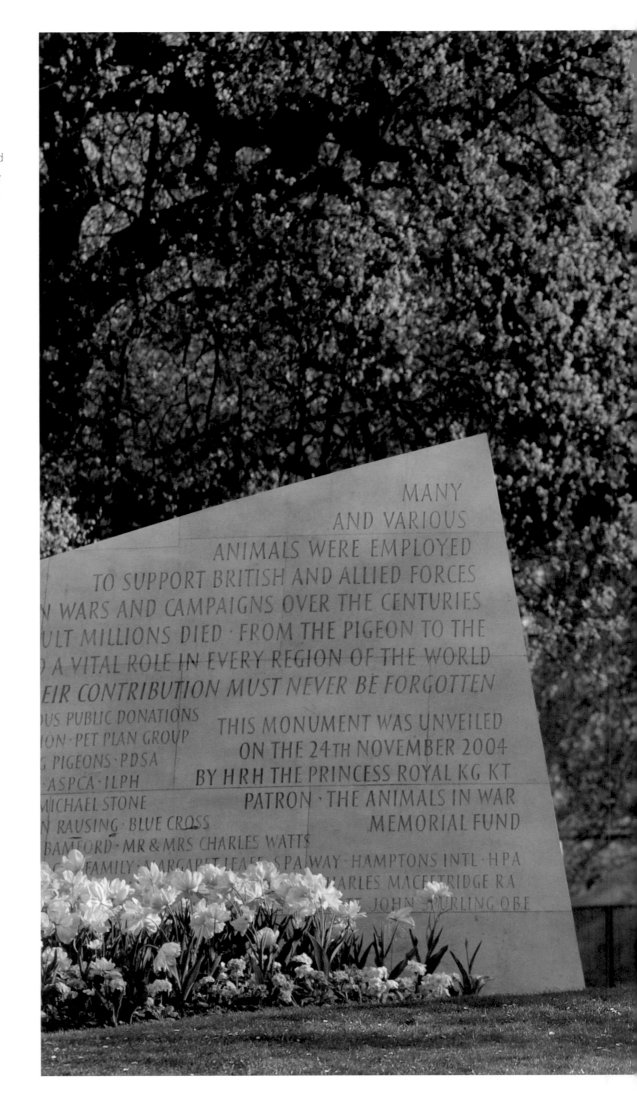

Above: Russian children in colourful costumes take part in the Pushkin in Britain Festival at Greenwich Park near Blackheath. It centres on a poetry competition involving Russian-language poets from around the world

Opposite: Rotten Row in Hyde Park has been one of the most fashionable places to ride horses in central London for over 300 years. The Park offers miles of bridleway and two outdoor riding arenas for more formal riding lessons and dressage. At 360 acres it is the same size as Monaco

Following page: Kayaks approaching Richmond-upon-Thames in the early morning mist

Above: This dawn view of Blackfriars Bridge with the cityscape in
the background resembles an 18th-century Canaletto painting

Following pages, left: Launched in 1869, the *Cutty Sark* was one of the last of the great tea clippers. In 1954 she was preserved as a museum ship in custom-built dry-docks at Greenwich. Seriously damaged by fire in 2007, she reopens in 2012

Right: David Wynne's gravity-defying *Girl with a Dolphin* sculpture (1973) stands on the bank of the Thames, north-east of Tower Bridge

Opposite: HM The Queen holds a traditional nosegay of flowers on Maundy Thursday at Westminster Abbey. Distributing Maundy Money to the needy or worthy on the Thursday of Holy Week dates back centuries. Recipients – in 2011, 85 women and 85 men, representing the Sovereign's age of 85 years – are all retired pensioners chosen for their work for the Church and their communities

Above: Peggy Scott, the Pearly Queen of Highgate, greets a Pearly King in Trafalgar Square on St George's Day 2011. The Pearly Kings and Queens are a charitable London tradition from the 19th century that originated when orphan street sweeper Henry Croft decorated his clothes with bright pearl buttons to attract money for charity

Above: The state-of-the-art entrance to Canary Wharf Underground station designed by Lord (Norman) Foster. This Jubilee Line stop serves the buzzing financial district and sees over 40 million people pass through it each year. Canary Wharf is also served by the Docklands Light Railway (DLR) and includes over 200 shops, waterside bars and restaurants

Previous pages, left: Viscount Linley, known professionally as David Linley, is founder of one of Britain's finest bespoke furniture marques and Chairman of auction house Christie's UK. He is a grandson of King George VI and son of the late HRH Princess Margaret, Countess of Snowdon, and Anthony Armstrong-Jones, the first Earl of Snowdon, acclaimed photographer and designer

Right: Lord (Sebastian) Coe in front of a 1475 painting by the Pollaiuolo brothers of *The Martyrdom of Saint Sebastian* (patron saint of athletes) in the National Gallery. Lord Coe won four Olympic Medals, including Gold for the 1500 metres in 1980 and 1984. He served as a Member of Parliament 1992–1997 and became a life peer in 2000. He headed the London bid to host the 2012 Olympics and is Chairman of the London Organising Committee for the Olympic Games and Paralympic Games (LOCOG)

Above: The 500-metre helical walkway winds its way through City Hall. Overlooking Tower Bridge, this is the home of the Mayor of London's offices and the London Assembly, and was designed to symbolise 'transparency' by providing views of the interior

Following pages, left: This iconic building by Norman Foster at 30 St Mary Axe, in the City, has transformed the London skyline. Nicknamed 'The Gherkin', it is seen here reflected on the bonnet of another prized English creation, a Jaguar car

Right: Not a job for the faint-hearted. These window cleaners are part of a specialist team that abseils down The Gherkin, washing all 744 windows as they go

A Docklands Light Railway train heads east from the Canary Wharf banking district at dusk. The sky-scrapers in the background show London's eminence as one of the world's leading financial centres. The dome of The O2 arena can be seen on the left

Lead singer Jon Bon Jovi fronts the Bon Jovi band, playing to a rapt audience at The O2 arena in London's Isle of Dogs opposite Greenwich Park

From rock to classical music: Bizet's opera *Carmen* is performed at The O2

Following page: British Tennis No. 1, Andy Murray, valiantly plays Rafael Nadal in front of a packed audience at The O2 in 2010. The arena is home to the ATP World Tour Finals, where the top eight players do battle. This giant venue seats some 20,000 people

Above: One of a team of runners that sped through Tate Britain's sculpture galleries every day for four months. The live performance, *Work No 850*, was devised by Martin Creed. Tate Britain houses a magnificent national collection of mainly British art since the 16th century

Opposite: Sunlight streams into the Turbine Hall at the Tate Modern, the acclaimed modern art museum in the former Bankside Power Station in Southwark – architect Sir George Gilbert Scott's 'Cathedral of Power.' Today it is the most visited modern art gallery in the world

Above: A saxophonist plays to passers-by on the rain-soaked flagstones of the South Bank near the Festival Hall

Opposite: White umbrellas make a decorative pattern on the Norman Foster-designed Millennium Bridge over the River Thames. St Paul's Cathedral, in the background, was designed by Sir Christopher Wren following the Great Fire of London of 1666

Above: Barcelona goalkeeper Victor Valdes and Manchester United striker Wayne Rooney take to the air during the 2011 European Champions League Final at the new Wembley stadium. Although Rooney later scored, Barcelona finally won this fiercely contested football match 3–1

Opposite: Rahul Dravid scores for India at Lord's during the first 2011 Test match against England. Lord's, founded by Thomas Lord in 1787, moved to St John's Wood in 1814. It is the 'home of cricket' and of Marylebone Cricket Club (MCC), which is regarded as the most prestigious cricket club in the world

Above: This little girl turned out to greet 'her hero', Major Packer, as he completed the Marathon in the Mall close to Buckingham Palace

Opposite: The inspirational Major Phil Packer MBE walks the London Marathon in aid of the Help for Heroes charity. Seriously injured in Afghanistan, he showed amazing bravery in completing the 26-mile course in two weeks on prosthetic legs and crutches. As he emerges from Tower Bridge, he is saluted by scarlet-coated Chelsea Pensioners and Beefeaters (Yeomen of the Guard – guardians of the notorious 11th-century Tower of London nearby)

Following pages: Members of the Southall Sikh community. Top left: London businesswoman, Surina Mangat. Below: Didier Singh Ranfhawa, Chairman of the Southall Sikh temple, Gurdwara Sri Guru Singh Sabha, one of the largest in the world (right)

Above: A gentleman catches up on the day's news in Pimlico

Opposite: Victorian-costumed cyclists with their penny-farthing bicycles at the annual Pimlico Road Party. In the background is Daylesford's popular organic food shop and café

Above: A small Jack Russell terrier at Battersea Dogs Home, the famous rescue and re-homing centre for dogs and cats. Behind is the dormant Battersea Power Station, now a listed building with plans for it to become a leisure and residential complex

Opposite: Cyclists pass St Paul's Cathedral during the Tweed Run: an organised ride through London. They dress in traditional British cycling attire. Started in London in 2009, the event has spread to cities worldwide

Following pages, left: The Palace of Westminster's clock face gets a clean. The clock and tower are often called 'Big Ben', but in fact the name was first given to the 13½-ton Great Bell installed in the tower in 1858. Its distinctive chime sounds on the hour and is broadcast twice a day by the BBC

Right: Ofra Zimbalista's *Blue Men* climb Maya House, Borough High Street

Above: A sugar ship at the Tate & Lyle refinery reminds us of East London's role as an important dock area. The piers of the Thames Barrier (centre) stand ready to protect London. One of the largest flood barriers in the world, it is seen here from the Woolwich Ferry at dusk

Previous pages, 72: 260 model elephants were placed across London for Elephant Family, the UK charity for wild and captive Asian elephants founded by writer-conservationist Mark Shand. Left: His sister HRH The Duchess of Cornwall and HRH Prince Charles at the Royal Hospital Chelsea

Page 72, right: Jack Vettriano's model in Burlington Arcade and green elephant at Westminster

Page 73, top: Celebration at 'Polo in the Park' at Hurlingham. Prince's Trust patron and keen polo sponsor, Saroj Chakravarty, plans to host an event for HM The Queen's Diamond Jubilee

Page 73, below: Kent & Curwen design the Hong Kong Olympic Team uniforms. Eric Kent and Dorothy Curwen founded the brand in 1926 as a purveyor of military and gentlemen's club ties. It has a long history with cricket, tennis and rowing and offers an essential wardrobe for the discerning

Refuelling at the Esso service
station near City Airport

Above: A drinks vendor at Somerset House sells cups of Pimms
No. 1, a staple British summer drink, at the open-air screening
of the film *Master and Commander* starring Russell Crowe

Opposite: Somerset House, a spectacular neoclassical building
between the Strand and the River Thames. Formerly home to
the Admiralty, today it hosts open-air concerts and films, and
contemporary art and design exhibitions. Here the audience
enjoys a live opera broadcast from Glyndebourne of Igor
Stravinsky's *The Rake's Progress* designed by David Hockney

Henry Wyndham, Chairman of Sotheby's, auctions in 2010 one
of the world's most expensive works of art ever sold: Alberto
Giacometti's *L'Homme Qui Marche I*. This 1961 piece, known
in English as *The Walking Man I*, sold for a record-breaking
£65,001,250

Pope Benedict XVI paid a four-day visit to the UK in 2010, when he addressed members of both Houses of Parliament in Westminster Hall. He was elected Pope at the age of 78, the oldest pontiff since Clement XII in 1730. In addition to his native German, he speaks several European languages and can read Latin, ancient Greek and biblical Hebrew

82

Above: India Ellis, aged five, with her horse from Hyde Park Stables in Bathurst Mews, which provides riding lessons

Opposite: Children play with hay on Southwark Bridge during the Thames Festival. The bridge is closed to traffic for an entire day and transformed into a land of eateries with locally grown produce and a festive supper with music

Previous pages, left: Ship's cat on the lookout

Right: Youngsters with their golden retriever on the family boat in St Katharine Docks. The Dock has been tucked away near Tower Bridge and the Tower of London since 1125. The modern Marina houses up to 200 luxury yachts and historic barges, with local pubs and shops

Opposite: The Very Reverend Dr John Hall, Dean of Westminster Abbey, somewhat unusually, has tea on the roof. He oversees the spiritual life of the mediaeval Abbey and provides ...rship to its 200 staff and 400 ...ers. The Abbey presents a ...ageant of British history – ...f St Edward the Confessor, ...monarchs, and count- ...has been the setting ...n since 1066 and ...ings, including the ...age of HRH Prince William ...Miss Catherine Middleton. The Abbey is neither a cathedral nor a parish church, but a 'Royal Peculiar' subject only to the Sovereign

Cleaner Available for work

I am a very honest cleaner looking for work. I have very good experience with cleaning ad if you are interested please call **Silvana** on 07447824900

Silvana, 07447824900

95

Opposite: Actress Sasha Waddell (right), who recently took a leading role in London in the world's longest-running play, Agatha Christie's *The Mousetrap*, takes tea with the author and psychotherapist Lucy Beresford in the graceful drawing room of the Draycott Hotel in Cadogan Gardens

Following page: Morton's private members' club in Mayfair's Berkeley Square has been part of the London social scene for 35 years. Owner Marlon Abela (centre), with his wife Nadya on his left, entertains guests. He is Chairman and founder of the Marlon Abela Restaurant Corporation. Morton's contemporary art collection features here Howard Hodgkin's *As Time Goes By*

These lucky diners in one of the London Eye capsules took part in the London Restaurant Festival's 'Pop-Up in The Sky'. They enjoyed a dramatic view over the Thames and the Houses of Parliament, also known as the Palace of Westminster, which was designed by Sir Charles Barry FRS (1795–1860)

Above: A delicious dish, almost too beautiful to taste.
Alain Ducasse's *tarte aux légumes* at his restaurant at
The Dorchester in Park Lane

Opposite: Entrepreneur Geoff Leong, at one of his restaurants
in Gerrard Street in London's Chinatown, surrounded by his
chefs who have prepared tantalising dishes of Chinese food

Following page: A Gold Medal display of vegetables from
Medwyn's of Anglesey at the RHS Chelsea Flower Show 2010.
The annual show, held in May by the Royal Horticultural Society
(RHS) in the grounds of the Royal Hospital Chelsea, is the start
of the 'Summer Season'

Above: Lupins, delphiniums and foxgloves in the Chelsea Physic Garden, which was founded in 1673 by the Worshipful Society of Apothecaries to train apprentices to identify plants and for botanical research

Opposite: A pretty English rose garden at a cottage on Ham Common

Previous page: The fascinating RBC (Royal Bank of Canada) New Wild Garden at the 2011 Chelsea Flower Show was designed by Nigel Dunnett

East London Business Alliance (ELBA) has facilitated photographic competitions and projects with East London schools since 2007. Over 500 students, including pupils from Tower Hamlets and Hackney, have been supported to deliver high-level images of the areas where they live. These are two of their photographs

Above: A typical Victorian East-End horse-drawn hearse, garlanded with flowers and dedicated to 'Mother', on its way to her funeral

Opposite: Marnie in a twirl

Following page: Aerialist Zahara O'Brien poses in the Palm House in May 2011 at the launch of the Kew Gardens Summer Festival. Kew is an internationally important botanical research institution with 700 staff and attracts millions of visitors. George III enriched the gardens, and in 1781 he purchased the adjoining Dutch House, now known as Kew Palace, as a nursery for the royal children

Buckingham Palace – flying the
Royal Standard flag to show that
HM The Queen is in residence –
overlooks Tiffany Fountain in the
Lake in St James's Park. Pelicans
have famously inhabited the Lake
since the 1660s when the Russian
Ambassador presented them to
Charles II

Above: Founder of Carol Joy London, Carol Hatton, at Ascot

Opposite: Guests in Carol Hatton's private box (No. 1) watch the races at Royal Ascot from the £200 million grandstand completed in 2006

Previous pages, left: Eccentric hatter David Shilling sports one of his top hat designs and his Royal Enclosure badge at Royal Ascot races. Young women have fun with their own creations

Right: HM The Queen arrives in traditional style at Royal Ascot. The world's most famous racecourse, its history spans 300 years from the reign of Queen Anne

Above: Aliya Itzkowitz (right), a member of the UK National Fencing Team,
competes in a spirited international sabre bout for cadets in Camden

Opposite: Seven-year-old Kechelle de Souza Dalton from Tottenham is
the youngest Karate Black Belt in the world. She has been training since
the age of three and does so five times a week in Belsize Park, Camden

Tamara Rojo, a Royal Ballet principal ballerina, and hip-hop dancers from the Urban Dance School join forces for the launch of the Cultural Olympiad of London 2012 Festival of Dance in the Floral Hall, Royal Opera House, Covent Garden

Above: Alan Campbell, Britain's leading single sculler. From 2006 to 2011 a finalist in the Olympics and every World Cup and World Championship (winning Silver and two Bronze Medals)

Opposite: Helen Jenkins is a British professional triathlete and the 2008 and 2011 ITU World Champion. Her Gold Medal in London in the 2011 World Championship Series secured her place at the London Olympics 2012

Following pages, left: Built in 1879, the Royal Arcade connects Old Bond Street with Albemarle Street in London's West End. It was given the 'Royal' prefix in 1882 when Queen Victoria bought her riding skirts and wool there

Right: City workers buy lunch in Leadenhall Market. Dating from the 14th century, it stands on what was the centre of Roman London. The ornate green, maroon and cream roof and the cobbled floors were designed in 1881 by Sir Horace Jones. It featured as the area of London near The Leaky Cauldron and Diagon Alley in the film *Harry Potter and the Philosopher's Stone*

Above: Young umpires at Wimbledon wearing elegant uniforms designed by Ralph Lauren

Opposite: Russian tennis star Maria Sharapova playing in the Ladies Final, which she lost to Petra Kvitova from the Czech Republic, at the 2011 Wimbledon Lawn Tennis Championships at the All England Lawn Tennis and Croquet Club

Above: Asprey's New Bond Street shop, with its fine new staircase, displays exquisite jewellery and handsome backgammon sets. Top of stairs: Jan-Erik Franck (left) with Stephen Dalziel of the Russo-British Chamber of Commerce. Below (left to right): Ivgenia Konovalova, Maria Dalziel, Sybil Stanislaus-Barrie

Opposite: The grand staircase of St Pancras Renaissance London Hotel is as dazzling as the day the hotel opened in 1873. The hotel was designed by Sir George Gilbert Scott

Following page: A big screen watched by thousands of people in Trafalgar Square shows HRH Prince William and Miss Catherine Middleton, now Duke and Duchess of Cambridge, en-route to Buckingham Palace from Westminster Abbey after their wedding on 29 April 2011. The bride's dress was designed by Sarah Burton at Alexander McQueen

Above: A model is made up for her catwalk appearance at London Fashion Week. London is one of the world's four major centres for high fashion

Opposite: A violinist, playing a violin encrusted with Swarovski 'crystals', serenades guests at the Help for Heroes dinner at The Dorchester hotel

Previous page: Mounted troopers from the Blues & Royals (Household Cavalry) stand guard outside The Dorchester. The hotel was host and a major sponsor of a fundraising dinner for the Help for Heroes charity

Above: Guy Kremer hair creation for the 2011 L'Oréal Professional Colour Trophy in London

Opposite: Last-minute adjustments before taking the stage at Vauxhall Fashion Scout, which showcases new talent

Opposite: Models reflected in the sunglasses on the British Fashion Council catwalk at Somerset House

Following pages, left: Models wait in the wings at a London fashion show

Right: Young men in Carnaby Street

Previous pages, left: A swan glides through the tranquil waters of the Thames near the ExCel Centre in East London. The international exhibition and convention centre is at a waterfront location in the heart of London's Royal Docks

Right: Alina Cojocaru, a principal dancer from Romania at The Royal Ballet, adopts a delicate swanlike pose. The Royal Ballet, founded in 1931, is based at the Royal Opera House, Covent Garden

Opposite: Christopher Foyle, his wife Catherine, broadcaster and author Giles Brandreth, and the actress Joanna Lumley (on table) share a joke with the CEO, Salem 'Sam' Husain, in Foyles' famous bookshop in Charing Cross Road

146

147

Above: 'The Little Girl with the Red Balloon' is said to be the work of the internationally renowned, anonymous graffiti artist, 'Banksy' – or is it?

Opposite: The Thames at low tide reveals all sorts of interesting creatures from eels (collected for sale by fishmongers) to this eccentric poseur. He relaxes on a chair he has constructed entirely out of specially imported sand . . . and he starts all over again after high tide!

Opposite: Jeremy Taylor, specialist in the British artists Edward Seago and Sir Alfred Munnings, with his wife Myra at their Stand at the British Art and Antiques Fair at Olympia Exhibition Centre, West Kensington

Above: Head Distiller Desmond Payne checks the quality of London's Beefeater gin at the distillery near the famous Oval cricket ground. The gin contains botanicals such as juniper, angelica, lemon peel, coriander, and Seville oranges. These ingredients are steeped in pure alcohol for 24 hours to give the gin its distinctive flavour

Opposite: Mark Webber, in the Red Bull Formula 1 racing car, sets off from Big Ben. On the left is Portcullis House, the new offices for Members of Parliament at Westminster

Below: London taxi and car line up by chance with an advertising poster showing British Olympic Gold Medal cyclist Rebecca Romero. She is only the second woman in history to win a medal in two different Summer Olympic sports – her first was a Silver for rowing

Following page: The National Gallery in Trafalgar Square. It houses one of the greatest collections in the world of Western European painting. Designed by William Wilkins, it was opened in 1838

Above: Skateboarding on the South Bank

Opposite: Jumping for joy in Portobello Road. The area's antique and bric-a-brac shops are beloved by tourists and Londoners alike

Following page, 158: Pigeon in the mist by Tower Bridge. Opened in 1894, Sir Horace Jones' famous bridge is 244m wide with two 65m towers. The two leaves of the central span can be split and raised in five minutes when river traffic needs to pass

Above: Elle Macpherson, businesswoman, TV host and exec-producer of Britain's Next Top Model, and supermodel known as 'The Body'. An Australian, she chooses to raise her two sons in London, which they call home. Elle continues her success with her own *Intimates* lingerie – one of the first crossovers between a model and a fashion label

Opposite: A craftswoman makes a wallet by hand at Ettinger, a luxury leather goods company based in Barnes. Founded by Gerry Ettinger 70 years ago, the company is still family-owned and run by his elder son, Robert. In 1996 Ettinger was granted a Royal Warrant by HRH The Prince of Wales

Above: Stamping a hallmark at the Assay Office, which is a key part of the Goldsmiths' Company, one of the City of London's Twelve Great Livery Companies. The Assay Office was founded in 1478 for compulsory testing of the quality and content of gold, silver and, today, platinum and palladium articles – and hallmarks them accordingly

Above: A young Old Tonbridgian gets a little help before dinner in tying his bow tie

Opposite: The annual Old Tonbridgian Dinner at Skinners Hall in the City of London. Sir Andrew Judd, a member of the Worshipful Company of Skinners, another of the City's Twelve Great Livery Companies, and a Lord Mayor of London, founded the school in Kent in 1553. The East India Company pioneers ventured forth in 1601 from this very hall, as is portrayed in the splendid panel (top near right) painted by Sir Frank Brangwyn

Above: Children enjoy a lesson in the Royal Institution (RI) Young Scientist Centre created by L'Oréal. Michael Faraday, the greatest RI scientist, initiated their popular Christmas Lectures in 1825

Opposite: In 2010 Nigerian Yinka Shonibare MBE created *Nelson's Ship in a Bottle* for the Fourth Plinth in Trafalgar Square. This scale model replicates Admiral Lord Nelson's flagship, *HMS Victory*, at the Battle of Trafalgar in 1805, during which Nelson was killed. The sails made from Dutch Wax textiles relate to African dress and identity. Nelson's Column to the right was completed in 1843

Following page: The Queen Elizabeth II Great Court at the heart of the British Museum is now enclosed under a glass and steel roof. At its hub is the former 1857 Reading Room, where those granted a reader's ticket included Mahatma Gandhi, Karl Marx, Lenin, George Orwell and Sir Arthur Conan Doyle. The Reading Room is now an exhibition centre and the books are at the new British Library in the Euston Road

Above: A fashionable collection of brightly-coloured shoes at a shop in Green Street Market in Newham, East London. This market has been a major shopping destination for the Indian community for many years

Opposite: A young woman chooses a wedding dress in a Green Street shop in Newham. Most of the 2012 Olympic Park is situated in this borough

Previous pages, left: Preparing for Notting Hill Carnival, the largest street festival in Europe. The area comes alive every August Bank Holiday with a parade, numerous sound systems and hundreds of Caribbean food stalls. Started in 1966 by the local West Indian community, the Carnival today attracts over one million revellers

Right: Two colourfully dressed performers at Notting Hill Carnival

Above: Baz, a well-known personality among the loyal clientele when he worked at this dry cleaners and repair shop in Pimlico

Opposite: A barber's shop on Brick Lane, in the East End of London, is now famous for its many curry houses. For centuries it has been a popular area among immigrant communities, starting with an influx of Huguenots in the 17th century. Today it is at the very heart of the Bangladeshi-Sylheti community

Following pages, left: One of Japanese bank Nomura's trading rooms in the City of London. The bank, founded in 1926, has an international network of some 27,000 people in more than 30 countries and provides a wide range of financial services

Right: One London Wall in the City of London, developed in 2004 and formerly owned by the Japanese construction company Kajima, is 13-storeys high and was designed by Foster + Partners. The building proudly stands on London Wall, the road that replaced the old Roman defensive wall

A statue of the late Sir Peter Scott at the Wildlife and Wetlands Trust Reserve in Barnes. The son of polar explorer 'Scott of the Antarctic', he was an eminent ornithologist, artist and founder of the WWT. Improvement of the Wetlands Reserve for the benefit of the public was facilitated by Berkeley Homes. Today one of the supporters is Royal Bank of Canada

Above: Catlin Commission winner Jasmina Cibic's *Bird Cage (after Pierre-Emile Legrain)*
at the Catlin Art Prize 2011 exhibition at The Tramshed in Shoreditch, East London.
The Prize supports the development of recent UK art graduates

Opposite: British Open Real Tennis Doubles Semi-Final at Queens Club in West London.
Steve Virgona and Nick Wood in the foreground at the Service End beat Camden Riviere
and Ben Matthews at the far side on the Hazard End. They went on to win the Final. Real
Tennis is the precursor to the modern game of Lawn Tennis and was originally played by
monks in the cloisters of monasteries in Italy and France. The name 'Real' is derived from
the French for 'Royal'. Real Tennis courts in England started at large country houses such
as Petworth and Hatfield, and Hampton Court where King Henry VIII played

Previous page: *Last Night of the Proms* – climax to the annual summer concerts founded by
Sir Henry Wood in 1895 at the Royal Albert Hall, Kensington. Jirí Belohlávek conducts BBC
Symphony Orchestra, as American soprano Renée Fleming, in a Vivienne Westwood gown,
delivers a stirring rendition of *Rule Britannia*. The audience wave Union Jack flags to music
by Thomas Arne and words by James Thompson

Prime Minister, the Rt Hon David Cameron MP, signs the Visitors' Book at the 2010 annual Lord Mayor's Banquet in the City of London's ancient Guildhall. His host was the then Lord Mayor of London, Sir Michael Bear (2010–2011). On right in traditional costume, stands a pikeman of the Honourable Artillery Company, Britain's oldest regiment, which was incorporated in 1537 by Royal Charter of Henry VIII

Opposite: Archbishop of Canterbury, Dr Rowan Williams (2nd from right), observes the Atash Nyaish ritual at the Zoroastrian Temple near Harrow as part of his mission to meet representatives of all the main religions practised in London.

Zoroastrians (Parsees) are 110,000 strong worldwide and have 6,000 devotees in the UK. Noted Parsees include the late Freddie Mercury of pop group Queen, Ratan Tata and Zubin Mehta

Following pages, left: Flaming leaves of the Chittamwood tree in autumn frame Temple of Bellona (a Roman war goddess) in Kew Gardens. It was designed for Princess Augusta by Sir William Chambers and built in 1760. The interior displays the names of British and Hanoverian regiments which distinguished themselves in the Seven Years' War (1754–1763)

Right: St Pancras Eurostar Terminal from the Renaissance London Hotel

Opposite: Rivals on land as well as water. Oxford University (dark blue) played Cambridge University (light blue) in 2010 in the annual rugby Varsity Match. The event began in 1872 and from 1921 has been held at Twickenham Stadium

Previous page: The 8th hole on Wentworth Golf Club's famous West course (called 'The Burma Road'). Wentworth was host to the annual World Match Play Championship from 1964 until 2007. Here a caddy (in white) fishes his client's golf ball out of the lake with a long-poled net. There are many lost balls at the bottom of the lake . . .

Following pages, left: Aerial view at dusk of the 80,000-seater Olympic Stadium, which will host athletics and the Opening and Closing Ceremonies at the London 2012 Games. As a lasting legacy, it will be used after the Games for sport, cultural and community events. Architects Populous designed the Stadium and developed the plans for the nearby venues of other Olympic sports

Right: The new Rolls Building off Fetter Lane in the City of London. It brings under one roof for the first time the Chancery Division, Admiralty & Commercial Court and Technology & Construction Court. Property group Delancey was a joint partner in facilitating its development as the largest specialist centre for the resolution of financial, business and property disputes anywhere in the world

Above: Shelagh Foyle, the principal perfumer at Floris, creates a new fragrance in the company's 'museum'. Floris has been family-owned through nine generations. Their Jermyn Street shop and offices were the family home when the company was founded in 1730. The firm holds several Royal Warrants

Opposite: Two Chairmen pub, a hidden gem on Dartmouth Street, Westminster, is minutes away from Winston Churchill's Cabinet War Rooms. The pub is so-named because customers were carried in sedan chairs by two chair men. Rebuilt in 1756, the pub still has exposed oak beams and a warm atmosphere to welcome locals and parliamentarians

Room with a view. This onefinestay flat on Albert Embankment looks out over the Houses of Parliament and (right) Lambeth Palace, 13th-century official residence of the Archbishop of Canterbury

Above: A pretty girl enjoys a cocktail made with Edgerton's pink gin in the cocktail bar of The Dorchester hotel. The pink colour is derived from pomegranates

Opposite: Peace and War. The 16,000 tonnes *Silver Cloud* luxury cruise liner ties up alongside wartime light cruiser *HMS Belfast* at Tower Bridge. The warship was opened to the public in 1971

Following pages, 208–209: The London Eye illuminates the night sky in this picture from Westminster Pier

Pages 210–211: Red deer in the snow in Richmond Park. Largest Royal Park in London, its royal links date from Edward I (1272–1307). The landscape has altered little and the Park is a National Nature Reserve and a Site of Special Scientific Interest

Opposite: The choirboys of the Chapel
Royal in their traditional red cassocks
hit the ice at Hampton Court Palace.
They are raising funds for choirboys'
music lessons and to refurbish the
chapel's historic organ

Previous page: Families tobogganing in
Richmond Park create a Lowry-esque
snowscape

Ice skating at Christmas time in the
elegant courtyard of Somerset House

Opposite: Regent Street Christmas lights make a charming pattern against the backdrop of the famous Dickins & Jones building, formerly owned by real estate group Delancey

Following page: Winter Wonderland. The Ferris wheel sparkles like a giant snow-flake in Hyde Park. One of London's Royal Parks, it is a 2012 Olympic venue

Below: Ho! Ho! Ho! Santas at Aldgate Underground station in the City. Members of Santacon on their way home. Each year they parade through the streets, sing-ing jolly Christmas songs, extending Christmas cheer and goodwill, giving small gifts to strangers

Eyes on a poster peep through a car on a crisp winter's day near St Thomas' Hospital

Acknowledgements

TONY BARRETT Tony is an outstanding photographer in his own right and has provided a number of photographs for the book. He has also been responsible for the digital and technical aspects of all the photographs. He has worked tirelessly and unflappably, overcoming the obstacles posed by my obsessive work style, and has been of great assistance to me in intuitively turning my vision into a reality.

PETER DRAPER Peter, also a talented photographer, has worked with me on location. He is a master of Photoshop.

GEORGE METCALFE George has been my editor for all my books and a friend for over 30 years. During that time he has cheerfully managed to put up with me.

EAST LONDON BUSINESS ALLIANCE Hazel Durrant, Culture Programme Manager, has been very supportive, allowing me to look at the ELBA picture library, for which I am most grateful.

DAVID OFIELD David is the Picture Editor of the *London Evening Standard*. He has provided a number of outstanding photographs for this book. David and his delightful wife Elizabeth have given me much excellent advice, over a glass of wine in the evening. I am much indebted to them.

LEO AMENDOLARA-BOURDETTE & STAFF AT MBE Leo has been an exemplary leader of the distribution team at Mail Boxes Etc in Wilton Road, Victoria, London.

DON MCGREGOR & JEAN JONES I give a big thank you.

FIGHT FOR SIGHT Faanya Rose is President and a Trustee of this charity, which funds pioneering research to prevent sight loss and treat eye disease. The charity holds an annual photography competition for photographs of London. Some winning pictures are in this book.

LIBANUS PRESS Michael Mitchell and Susan Wightman for their brilliant work imposing the photographs and the text for the final layout of the book.

THE COLOURHOUSE Trevor Buck and his team for their marvellous printing of this book. Bound by Hunter & Foulis.

PANASONIC *LUMIX* This compact camera has taken a number of excellent photographs for this book.

CAROLINE MEYER Caroline, in exchange for regular cups of tea, has given great advice on the text and captions.

EMI IKEBE Emi (below) has given me endless support.

PAULINE LLOYD Last but by no means least, Pauline is the person on whom I heap the highest praise. An extraordinary PA, who is totally loyal and who has been unstintingly dedicated to the project. She has masterfully overseen the text and captions and worked by phone far into the night, frequently being back on duty at 8 o'clock the next morning to deal with the mountain of correspondence. I cannot thank her enough.

I should also like to mention the excellent support given in so many different ways, first and foremost by Zed Cama, but also by Sybil Stanislaus-Barrie, Paul Phillips, Alan O'Sullivan, Julie Ronald, Jan-Eric Franck, Edmond Fenton, the Hon Alex Foley, Bill and Iwona Barry, Nick Salaman, Caroline Newton, Rebecca, Lizzy Glassford and Martin Gill.

Chelsea Pensioner Margery Cole in an Eagle E-Type Jaguar (arranged by Michael Scott and Ewan Warrender) at the Royal Hospital Chelsea

First published in Great Britain in 2012 by
The Beautiful Publishing Company Limited
Wickham House, 464 Lincoln Rd, Enfield, EN3 4AH

Text © Anthony Osmond-Evans 2012
Design & layout © The Beautiful Publishing Company Ltd 2012

Paper: Novatech matt from Antalis-McNaughton

www.TheSpiritofLondon.com